Deep I

Sophia Michaels

I dedicate my first book to my friend Nita. I have known her since I was six years old. We have fought, and made up, and always been friends.

I also acknowledge my dear husband for putting up with listening to me reading my new works at midnight.

And my brother for giving me the spirit to go on.

Deep I

Sophia Michaels

BRAISWICK
111 High Road East,
Felixstowe, Suffolk IP11 9PS
www.braiswick.com

ISBN 1 898030 72 3

British Library Cataloguing in Publication Data available.

Cover illustration by Hayley Jayne

Printed in England by Lightning Source
Braiswick is an imprint of Catherine Aldous Design Ltd

To Phil

The Christmas comes
The Goose gets fat.
Eat, Drink & Be Merry.

Enjoy my words and
work. Happy Christmas

Love

Sophia

Michaels
x x

21/12/2005.

Poems

Cat
Clara   2
Black Eyes   3
Serenity   4
Kim She   6
Jet   7
The Cat   8

For Us All
The Children Stood   10
Communication - Style   12
Don't   13
Judgement   14
The Box in the Corner   15
The Cross Around Neck 16
These Are The Pictures   17
What's The Question   18
Us   21
A Town Called Debt   22

Looking Back
Dedicated to George   24
Moment   25
Disco   26
Stories In Photographs   28

Looking Forward
Corridor   31
This Day   32
Only 15 Years   33
Yesterday   34

Love
A Crowded Space   36
A Thousand Beats   37
A Letter As Promised   38
Breasts Of Day   40
Breeze   42
I can't help the way   43
Dangerously Beautiful
Colours   44
If I   46

Ironic   47
In The Day Of The Night 48
Linger   50
Love Comes   51
Love   52
Making Love   53
Lady of the Fake   54
My Sleeping Beauty   56
There You Stood   57
Why?   58

Melancholy
But Flowers   60
Destiny   61
Company Of Hover Flies 62
Of Late   63
I've Seen   64
Out Of The Window   65
Sing and Sigh   66
This Life Has No Title   68
We Are All But Flowers   69

Miscellany
In Any Street   71
Pills   72
Similar Person   74
Pen To Paper   76

Mother Love
A Mother's Lot   78
Mother   80
Eternal   82
Gifts To A Child   83
Tea Time   84
My Boy   86

Old Age
A Place Of Old Things   88
Old Men   90
Now   92
Remote   93

One Life Only
Are You Where You Want
To Be   95
Debate Debate Debate 96
Burning   98
Don't Steal My Dreams 99
Every Enjoyable Puff   100
How Many Times   101
Knock On The Door   102
Knocked Down   103
The Telly   104
No   105
The Fat In My Fridge 108

Our Planet
A Simple Answer   111
Black Dawn   112
The Perfect World   114
Black Shore   115
Lights on the Landscape 116
The War Machine   118
The Animals in the Zoo 120
Man Will Eat The Fish 122
To Some Men 123
Wise Words   126

Sadness
He Moves Beside You 128
In Slumber   129
My Friend   130
Sun-kissed   131
On Going To My Best Friend's
Grave   132
The Bloom   134
Walking In The Wild Wind 135
The Human Touch   136

Time
Buy Time   138
Copper Days 139
Fragments Of Time 140
I See   142
Only Form   143

Slow   144
Take Time   145

Wild Nature
Fly On The Wall 147
Rain All Day   148
Storm Calm 149
The Land By The Sea 150
The Sea   152
The Snow Flake 154

Woman
A Poem For Me 156
A Woman's Day 157
In A Woman's Eyes 158
A Woman's Fullness 160
The Womb Within 161
Rosebud   162
Transform   164

Sophia has lived in Suffolk for much of her life. She was brought up on a council estate by hard-up hard-working parents, where to have sweets was utter indulgence. However, since a young age Sophia has always looked upon life as an interesting journey rather than a humdrum existence and sought to make the best of whatever opportunities are offered. Her philosophy is to instil in people that there is more to life than just work, and that you must live life to understand that there is always more, not forgetting that time passes quickly.

For many years she has had a keen interest in poetry either, reading or writing. She has studied William Shakespeare, Charles Dickens, and her favourite poet, John Keats. In future Sophia plans to continue to study her favourite poet, and to produce many more books of poetry.

Deep I, is a modern observation of daily humdrum life, mixed together with the feelings that 'live in my soul' spilled out on paper. This light-hearted book is relatable and funny, and thought fully different. Covering many subjects from darkness to light, and the humorous, which will keep the reader of this easy-to-read poet interested from one page to the next.

Cat

Clara

She never liked anyone
She never liked her friends
She never liked the rats and birds
She never liked the hens
She never liked the dogs or mice
Nor the visiting lice
In fact, she hated one and all
This black pussycat;
Who sat all day so serenely looking my way
Staring at me with those treacherous eyes
That flickered now and then
with the movement of the flies.
'Where's my food?' she meowed so rude,
'And fresh milk?' she purred like silk
Waiting patiently for the plates and bowls to descend
Like flying saucers from above to the floor
Where she will have her feast
Then be out the door.

Black Eyes

Black eyes
Watching me
Stirring me
Alluring me.
Black eyes
Looking through me
Willing me
Enchanting me.
Black eyes
Tempting me
Caressing me
Deceiving me.
Black eyes
Staring me out of my good intention
Haunting me
Betraying me.
Black eyes
Stroking me with their velvet expression
Kneading me.
Black eyes
Feeding me
With all their emotion.
Black eyes
Never leaving me.
Black eyes
Greedy for me
Hungry for me.
Black pussy cat eyes
Always, so full of cunning lies.

Serenity

Serenity is the cat's name
Serenity is the cat's game.
Serenity the one that fools
Serenity the one that mauls.
Serenity the one that has to crunch
Serenity the one you never think has had lunch.
Serenity who loves to eat
Serenity loves to cheat.
Serenity so serene
Serenity the one you think is such a dream.
Serenity the one you love to stroke

Serenity the one you wish you could choke.
Serenity the one with her coat so smooth
Serenity the one with the power to soothe.
Serenity the one that loves
Serenity the one that feels like a silk glove.
Serenity the one you love to kiss
Serenity the one with the will not to miss.
Serenity must have everything
Serenity shall make your heart sing.
Serenity will make you want to cry
Serenity will make you want to ask why.

Serenity with the will to win
Serenity with the will to sin.
Serenity so slick
Serenity so quick.
Serenity say's, 'I love my life'
Serenity say's, 'I do not have strife'.
Serenity the one so mean
Serenity the one so clean.
Serenity the masterful player
And all she wants you to do is
obey her.

Kim She

She came in the other night
She was rather late
She was lucky
She did not get shut out
She came in her usual self

She the one so full of confidence
She the one so full of life
She the one who inflicts the terror
She the one who gives the ultimate pleasure
She the one I love so much

She the one I love to touch
She the one I am forever calling
She the one who has no responsibility
She the one with haughty elegance
She the one so sleek and slick

She the one who files her nails on a stick
She the one who makes no sound, yet
She has the purr-fect voice, and
She knows I know her choice
She the one who will have her way

She the one who understands; yet
She will not listen
She the one who coils and snakes herself about my legs
She the one who looks then says,
"My life is full of purr-fect comforts."

6

Jet

I am the cat,
The Jet black cat
You can be sure of that.
All day I sit on the window sill
And she ignores me still.
"What next" I say to myself,
As I walk around the objects on the shelf.
"How can I get her to stroke me,
And sit me on her knee,
Ah, I have the very thing,
That will make her sing.
'I'll purr, and purr, and purr, and purrrrrrrrrrrrr,
Until she strokes my
Fur, and fur, and fur, and furrrrrrrrrrrrr.'

The Cat

Stroking the shiny cat
Sliding my hands over his silken back
A pleasure it is to behold;
His slick sleekness
And charming serenity
His strong will
And bold attempts
At making me do
What only he can invent,
For he has this power over me
That draws me in and in
In to what I thought was his conscious mind
Only to be awoken
By his sudden lack of interest
And by the lies
That always hide behind those penetrating eyes.

For Us All

The Children Stood

And there the children stood
With arms outstretched
Wanting a bowl full of love and food
And food and love and a hug
And a shelter
And a roof.

But all they got and had
Were bowls full of emptiness and wanting
Bowls full of misunderstanding
Bowls full of nothing but pain and injury
Bowls full of empty promises
And some times even lies.

Bowls full of big sad eyes
Bowls full of tears that cried
Bowls full of haunted expression
Bowls full of good intention
Bowls full of newspaper articles and bulletins
Between plentiful commercials.

Bowls full of souls that died
And hearts that were broken.
And there the children stood
With arms outstretched
Waiting Waiting Waiting
Ps: with plenty of patience.

Response:

And now I look at my
Silver bowls
Plastic and stainless steel bowls
Fruit and soup bowls
In a different light
Knowing now that I understand the children's plight.

Communication - Style 2004

Picture it
Send it
Receive it
Laugh at it
Reply to it
Text it
Phone it
Email it
Fax it
Communicate it
Mobile it
Lap top it
Pc it
Land line it
Satellite dish it
Cable it
Wireless it
Morse code it
Binary code it
Triangulation it
Computer navigation it
Landing control it.

Don't

Don't send the children to bed
With tears in their eyes.
Don't send them to bed
With their hearts full of cries.
Don't send them to bed
With questions full of why's.
Don't send them to bed,
With their feelings all knots and ties.
It doesn't take much to understand how they feel,
Even if at times they do act unreal.
It doesn't take much to remember that these little
people
Will always love you,
And to you they will always be true.

Judgement

What ever you do
Good or bad
Will come back to you
It will hit you smack bang
On the face
Come right up to your front door
And dump itself on the floor.

It may take a few years
You might cry a few tears
Require a few hushes
Cover up a few blushes.
So, before you come knocking at my door
Just open your cupboard
And watch the skeletons tumble out on your floor.

The Box in the Corner

I am the box in the corner
I am the box that steals your dreams
I am the box that steals your senses
I am the box that shows you all
Yet, reveals not a thing of the truth
I am the box you can take with a pinch of pepper
Or a grain of salt.

I am the box
Of which your intelligence I shall insult
I am the box that shows you all you want
All you could need
And all you could have
Yet, you cannot touch or feel it,
Because it is not real.

The Cross Around My Neck

I may not call upon the Lord that often
But I think of him every day
Because I wear the Cross around my neck
And because I wear the Cross around my neck
I think therefore of him every day.
And today I call upon his strength
To get me through this maelstrom of a difficult time
To calm me
To bring peace into my life.

Amen

These Are The Pictures

Draw me a picture of the worlds you have inside
You know, the ones you are always trying to hide
From people who will never understand you
Or realise life them selves.
These are the pictures that flourish
With no one beside to appreciate
What they really mean
The pictures you think
Will only ever be a dream.
These are the pictures you deny and hide every day
Hoping that perhaps they will eventually die and fade
way
Not so.
Because once a dream
Always a dream
And a dream is dreamt with precision
Eventually to become a vision
At your behest
But, you have to make that decision.
Draw me a picture of the worlds you have inside
The ones you are always trying to hide
The ones in life you have so far denied.

What's The Question

What's a life
What's a wife
What's a child
What's the man.
What's the question
What's the answer.
What's a slice of laughter
What are you after
What's it all for.
What's a lover
What's a mother
What's a father
What's the truth
What's a lie.

What's the why
What's the how
What's the here
What's the now.
What's the present
What's the future
What's the past
What's the last
What's the first.
What's the difference
What's the same.
What's the player
What's the game.
What's the prayer

What's the dream
What's the vision
What's the decision.
What's the expectation
What have you got.
What's the yet
What's the nearly
What's the lost
What's the found.
What's the can
What's the can't.
What's the realistic
What's the not.
What's a leaf upon a tree

What's a dead bird on the ground.
What's the displeasure
What's the comfort.
What's the need
What's the greed.
What's the silver
What's the gold
What's in the pot
What's your lot
What's the dross
What's your loss
What's your aim
What's your gain
What's your pain.

What will this all mean to you when it is put together
What will it say to you
What will it bring to mind
What meaning in it will you find
What's out there
What's the ultimatum
What's to share.
What's your voice
What's your choice.
What's your state
What's your fate.
What in you will my words shake.
What feelings in you will my words awake.
What's the question?

Us

God gave us only one life
He never gave us two
He gave us dreams and inspiration
He showed us what he wanted us to do
He showed us the road on which to travel
He gave us the path to unravel
He wanted us to please him
By helping and encouraging others
By showing them that they too could become someone
And something.
He showed us a bird high on the wing
He showed us freedom
And what it all meant.
He didn't want our wasted lives spent
In frustration
And procrastination.
He wanted us to see the glory and the light
Whether it be the day or night.
He wanted us all to be special
And to feel good about what he wanted us to do
He wanted us all to be true to ourselves.
But most of all
He wanted us to win.

A Town Called Debt

Do you live in a town called debt?
Is the place you live in called your own?
Or does it belong to some one else
Namely the bank manager?

Do your mortgage repayments keep his wife
in diamonds, fast cars, and tropical holidays?
Do you sleep at night,
Or do you stay up all uptight?

A millstone around your neck,
That's what it is.
A servant to the lender,
That's what you'll be

As soon as you go into debt.
So stay out of debt my friend,
If you can pay for your house
On the one payment plan.

Looking Back

Dedicated to George, 1983

Encounter the wind
For it has the strength to whip through your mind.
It can change your lifestyle
With such completion.
If you let it
If you dare.

Think of the crisp white snow underfoot
It is clean, it is pure
Live in the crystal clear harmony
The white velvet is smooth unruffled,
And so too should be your mind.

Think of the rain when there are tears
They will not last too long
For when the grey clouds decide to go yonder
You may look to the sky with a crystal clear eye;
Life itself has always sparkled, glistened and gleamed,
But you have never seen.

Encounter the wind
For it is strong
And so to is your mind.

Love from Sophia xx

Moment

I want that moment
To be here now
Though I have no wish to wish
The moment away
For the moment passes quickly enough
But, Ah,
How I want that moment to be here now.

Disco

It's funny how a song can bring on a thought and a
feeling
Felt by no one else with all feelings reeling.
A song a melody that takes you back
To that song track
And where you were
And where you were
At
Some night years ago
Loving your partner
Smooching at the disco

With all lights swirling on the floor
And at that moment you had just discovered life's
shore
A paradise
In the dry ice,
Enveloped by a mist;
You were kissed.
So lovingly, intensely, beautifully, hauntingly
While you saunteringly
Gave all with your closed eyes in imagination
And flirtation.

In the hot sweaty smoky dimness
Of sexual expectation
Your groin in gyration,
You felt the need,
And only the need
Without commitment
Briefly only a moment;
Was all that was needed
At the disco
For you to moan and let go!

Stories Like This Are Only Told In Old Photographs

Where the hell has that time gone
The time captured in that photograph
The one I just pulled from the draw
The one where I wore the backless dress
(I think I've still got it upstairs somewhere)
Trying to impress the blokes I suppose
Who eyed me up
And down.
Where the hell has that time gone?

Was it so long ago?
I can't remember the celebration.
Was it my brother's twenty first,
Or my sister's eighteenth.
My mother had a habit of putting two parties together.
I do remember though that the ceiling was too low
Because the cigarette smoke lingered all night like a
thick fog,
Hanging over the sandwiches, vol au vent,
And every passive smoker.

The evening wore on, the drinks flowed
And the heads got thicker
With the effects of the booze
The senses and judgement became less guarded.
The music reverberated around the walls

Seeming to bash out our eardrums.
The dancing began,
Hips started swaying in provocative mood,
Gyrating groins in movements so rude.

Not a thing was left to the imagination.
The night wore on and so did the booze
Begin to have the desired effect.
Eyes that shouldn't met, looking a little deeper,
Into perhaps more than was good for us
The windows of the soul were opened
And all was revealed
At last; secrets were exposed
Now, the conquest was fulfilled.
Stories like this are only told in old photographs.

Looking Forward

Corridor

Wizened old men
With wrinkles deep
Fall onto the floor
In a fleshless heap.
Scarred by the many turbulences in life
Deep in remorse now; with no "enduring" wife.
Their days are out numbered, out shone
The darkness from now on will greet them before
long,
Then it will all seem like the end of book,
 chapter and verse
And as empty as the voice that 'far off' seems to echo
from (a) nurse, from
Somewhere back along the 'far reaching' corridor.

This Day

This day
Is a sunny day
A bright day
A really lovely day
A beautiful day
An all you could ever wish for day
A marvellous day.

A magnificent day
A rare kind of day
A truly glorious day
A special day
An optimistic day
But this is what life is all about.

It's about accepting the rainy
Horrible grey days
The miserable damp dull days
The days that seem endless
And appear to drag on into next week
And never want to go away
With the same appreciation.

Response, it makes the flowers grow.

Only 15 Years

15 years old
I wish that I were 30
I don't want to reach 45,
Now, I am 45
I am only 15 years away from 60
But still only 15 years away from 30,
Now, I am 60
I am only 15 years away from 75
But still only 15 years away from 45,
Now, I am 75
I am only 15 years away from 90
Wishing that I were nearer 45, or 60.
Now, that I am 90
I am only 15 years away from 105.
Now, shall I go on.

Yesterday

Yesterday he wanted to be an astronaut
Today he wants to be an FBI agent
The day before yesterday he wanted to be a scientist
Then tomorrow he'll want to be an inventor.
Last week he said "You remember mummy, I told you
I wanted to be a pop-star
And next week I want to fly a plane,
But before we do all this mummy
Can we go to Australia?
This is the stuff that dreams are made of
The stuff where dreams come from
The stuff we dream about when we are kids
Then later we put aside all those dreams we have
inside
Saying we'll get around to living them someday
And that day was yesterday.

Love

A Crowded Space

I've been across a road
A street
A crowded room
And seen your face
And your body
The face of the body
I've never had
The face of the body I always wanted
But as yet I've never had
But I will
But for now
My wonderings are still.

I'll know the moment your eyes strike mine
The moment their mirror reflects mine
The moment that smile plays about them
Then, their innermost thoughts will be revealed to me.
I've seen your body and your face
Across a road, a street
And the pleasure that passed came and ended all too
soon
For I could not get across that crowded space
I could not get a moment
To caress and glide my fingers across your face
I wanted to
But, there was between you and me too much in the
way.

A Thousand Beats

As I stand before yourself
And set my eyes upon your face
My heart begins to beat at a thousand mile pace
And then the pain in my chest is all too real
And then am I wounded
And feel then, like I have this howling animal living in
my veins
Wanting to escape the never-ending torment
As my love for you seems locked in this cage
Never able to get out
And yet, at the same time it is being fed;
It is

Never allowed to see the sun
Never allowed to let its wild heart run
Over the moors, the hills, and vales,
Over the glens, the valleys, and dales,
Over the seas, the rivers, and streams,
This is how my sad heart screams;
For you to love me
But this is just a perfect illusion
Creating in me utter confusion
And as I set my eyes upon your face
You again, disappear.

A Letter As Promised

Every time I leave you,
I want you more,
Every time I want you more
I wish that I did not.
Every time I ask and want you
To want me more,
I wish that I had never asked
Or made the mere suggestion,
Because every time I want you more,
It appears to me that you do not want me more,
Then every time you reject me
Then, I am, sorely hurt;
To the bottom of my feelings that live within my body:
Crying out for you to love me more,
But I wish that I did not.

I love you more than the sun that loves my skin
But wish that I did not.
I love you more than the flowers need the rain
But wish that I did not.
I love you more than the snow blanketing the
mountain top
But wish that I did not.
I love you more than a caressing wind on my face
But wish that I did not.
I love you more than more than love itself
But most of all
I hoped and wished that I did not.
But, I, will love you always
For as long as the picture of your face lives in my head
But, most of all,
I wish that I did not.

Breasts Of Day

I cup my swollen breasts
To rub the pain away
These are the breasts that boys drunk from
Then off to the battle field they went and come
Far and far away
Thinking of breasts that excite
That comfort and pleasure.
These breasts are the breasts of love
Swollen with pride
For the new bride and her groom.

Her swollen breasts give him all he has ever had
All he has ever looked for
For all the pleasure he has ever known
And sought
His moments are one and the same
As they have ever been
Pink skin, a beauty to behold,
His mother, his wife,
Being all together in a gold wedding band
Softness anew.

Yet, the same sensations rule the day
His beautiful night of charm and lace
His caressing hands, and searching mouth
Doing all they have ever done and wanted.
And now the bride cups her swollen breasts
On the light of day
Then waits for her man lover
To love her one and only
No mother and no more,
For all woman is alike to him.

Breeze

I'll never forget that face
His face
Those enchanting eyes
They left me with a warm embrace.
I'll never forget that touch
His touch
I want to
I need to.
Yet I still crave for those fleeting caresses
And wondrous feelings.
I'll never forget his breath upon my brow
It was like a tropical breeze.
I'll never forget those many nights
As the moonlight cast lacy shadows on my bedroom
wall
I want to forget it all
I need to.
I'll never forget his warmth
It left me trembling conquered
Aflame in paradise
Was this his aim?
Or was I the game?
I'll never forget any of this
Though I must forget it all.
I'll never forget the longing for the comfort
Only he can bring.

I can't help the way I feel about ya

I feel as wild as the horses that run by the sea
As wild as the wind that blows into me
As wild as the snow that softly falls onto me
As wild as the rain that pelts onto me.
As wild as the sea that crashes onto the shore
As wild as the moon on a tidal wave.
As wild as an animal trapped in a cave
As wild as a young indian brave.
As wild as the rivers that flow down the falls
As wild as a storm that frightens and takes all.
As wild as my thoughts that will be remembered to
the grave
As wild as those intimate moments you gave.
As wild as those heavenly moments in mysterious
silence
As wild as the heat of the suns violence.
As wild as the storm in the heat of the night
As wild as the child flying a kite.
As wild as the flaying hail against a fence
As wild as a woman that has no defence.
As wild as the stars that shoot around the sky
As wild as thoughts that run in my head and ask why.
As wild as a serene cat purring at ya
I can't help the way I feel about ya.

Dangerously Beautiful Colours

The dangerously beautiful colours
Are all lies to our eyes.
The deceptive creations entice
Fanciful hindering involvement,
That's yours alone, not mine.

Flippancy flourishes in you,
But seriousness is what I need of you.
You float upon your iced blue sea,
I lie upon the intense red,
And hell you still enter my head.

I see fire, and what do you do
With your iced blue,
You dampen my intense red,
Until I am practically dead, Then you grip my arm
Enticing me to those heavenly white clouds.

Blissful, intense red is what I now see for me,
But for you it's still the iced blue,
Now it's my turn
To turn grey,
Because you say I must stay away.

I rise, the lightning strikes,
Thunder bolts through my heart.
It crackles,
An electric blue now enters your head.
Surely you must want me anything but dead?

Your sentiments are strong indeed,
Resolute you now must be,
You shall see,
I will redeem all
You have taken from me.

But now you are dead,
So too is my intense red.
And I shall never, forever, let
Dangerously beautiful colours again
Enter my head.

If I

If I had loved you
A little too much the other day
I would not be able to love you
As much as I do today.

Ironic

It's ironic, is it not
That you should laugh
And I should not.
Through the pain and the hate
Through the love and the grace
It's ironic, is it not
That you should laugh
And I should not.

In The Day Of The Night

A magic morning
A superb dawning
An interesting awakening
My senses all a glowing
My body now
To-ing and fro-ing
My thrusting hips
My wanton lips
Waiting for kisses
My silken skin enjoying
With a will to win;
All that I desire
My passion
My flames
Within
Getting higher
Getting hotter
Now I want needing
Now I need kneading
Slowly
Deeply
Lovingly.
Flowing now
Gushing now

Heaven
And beauty now
Stars
And firmament now
Together up there
In the air
We are one now.
Sun shine now
Birds song now
Morning now.

Linger

Let me gaze upon your face
A few seconds longer
That I may remember it a moment longer.
Let me remember your touch
Even though at times it was all too much
Though in reality it was never enough.
Let me stand before your self a second longer
That I may smell the scent of you
So that its power and presence will linger
Forever, in myself.

Love Comes

Love comes in many shades
Pale and pink
Delicate and fragile
Nevertheless it comes
Hot and ferocious
Red and fiery
Love comes as soft as silk
To the touch
Of faint kisses
And caresses the brows of many lovers.

Love

If a minute were an hour
And an hour a day
A day a week
A week a year
A year a century
A century a thousand years
My love for you would last forever
In amongst the stars
In a far off sparkling constellation

Making Love

Making love
Is like making lace
It has to be intricately interwoven
To form an everlasting pattern
Then placed in the most precious of places.

Lady of the Fake

I am the lady of the fake
Fake tan
Fake man
Fake tits
Fake lips
Fake waist
Fake nails
Fake smiles
Fake eyes
Fake dreams
Fake money
Fake ideas
Fake tears
Fake hopes
Fake hair
Fake care
Fake bank account
Fake amount
Fake impression
Fake depression
Fake perfume
Fake penthouse rooms
Fake words
Fake, fake absurd
Fake actress
Fake dress
Fake glove
Fake love

Fake knots and ties
Fake lies
Fake gain
Fake pain
Fake price
Fake nice.
I am the lovely lady of the Fake.

My Sleeping Beauty

As the morning dew slides over the land
I wish I could take my lover's hand
But alas he sleeps entwined in heaps of sheets
Curled up somewhere beneath
Making a dreadful noise
Like a pig through his snout
And each time I jab his ribs and shout
I get the same reply
What's the matter? murmured through closed lips
You're snoring
You old snore bag.

There You Stood

I thought that this was my lot
Everything was pucker.
Then I walked into the room
And saw your face,
And
I was stopped in my tracks;
As your smile slapped itself across my heart
Where the real feelings start
Flinging open wide the emotion

Which before was hidden from view
Where unfulfilled passion was driven
To hide in some dark place
To never show itself upon my face.
And now I've not seen you for ages
Though still am I full of great expectation.
And, as there you stood, just within my grasp
in the light, but still hidden away from my view,
As usual.

Why?

You touched,
But you did not feel.
You looked,
But you did not see.
You loved,
But you did not love.
Why?

Melancholy

But Flowers

We are all but flowers
We seed
We germinate
We grow
We bloom
We feel the warmth of the sun
We feel the pelting cold rain
We wither
We seed
We die
We shrivel
We compost
We replenish
We are all but flowers.

Destiny

In my work
I can hide in it
I can escape in it
I can be me in it
And my destiny becomes my business.

In my walking
I can hide in it
I can escape in it
I can be me in it
And my destiny becomes my business.

In my bathing
I can hide in it
I can escape in it
I can be me in it
And my destiny becomes my business.

In my loving
I cannot hide in it
I cannot escape in it
I cannot be my self in it
And then my destiny is in question.

In The Company Of Hover Flies

Hover flies
Surround my immediate sky
The space
Between me
And there
The place
Where the sun creeps in
To warm my pale skin
To warm my bones
To encourage a sense a well being
In the late late spring;

With everything that flies around
And the creatures that come out of the ground
The sight of them warms my heart
And enriches my mind with thoughts
Of the summer yet to come
Now, I know at last winter is done.
The apple tree shall once again bare fruit
And flowers shall dazzle
Each and every eye that gazes upon them.
But, for now I shall and be
In the company of hover flies.

Of Late

Of Late
My life's
Full of
Strife
Heartache
Pain
Frustration
Anger
But of late
I have learnt to get over these trials
And traits
To accept
My fate.

I've Seen

I've seen that smile a thousand times
But now it nothing means
It meant
It could
Have been
And had
And seen
Given
Shared
Loved
But no
It lied
Beyond all lies
To
Keep a life of misery
As misery in the music is played
As prominent as the play acted
Is displayed
Timed to its short life.
And now like mine
As I stare and sit
To observe and watch
And parallel the play
In which before my eyes
Unfolds about me
Like my one life
Into a thousand
Billion civilisations
Forever and forever
Dawning.

Out Of The Window

Out of the window the inspiration will come
Out of the window when the day is glum.
Out of the window I'll fling wild thoughts away
Out of the window to look at another day.
Out of the window my sadness will fly
Out of the window high in the sky.
Out of the window my melancholy will pass
Out of the window through the pain and glass.
Out of the window I will see a glorious sunset
Out of the window through blurred vision, remorse
and perhaps regret.
Out of the window I'll discard those things of which I
prefer to leave in the back of my mind,
Out of the window to unravel and unwind.
Out of the window all of the time
Out of the window natures clock stands to chime.
Out of the window there could a small pleasure be,
Out of the window waiting just for me.

Sing and Sigh

Swallows gather on a wire
Waiting to go on the wing
To swift like acrobats round the sky
Twittering all the time with great excitement
In anticipation
Of the impending incredible journey,
Which takes each tiny beautifully created bird
Half way round the world
To some bright hot and sunny place.

The fragile body, and
Sleek plumage
Belie its inner strength
And capabilities.
Admired by the layman
The preacher
And the pilot
It inspires the artist
And lures the poet, and
leaves us
Wishing, wanting, and longing
For summer days just gone by;
And in the realisation
That winter waits just up ahead.

My heart sings and sighs in the same moment
As I see these little birds set to gather
In the October's chilly mists.
Tomorrow,
I shall wake to hear the silence in the skies
The noise of yesterday gone.
One day
Soon
The Spring time will, erupt
My friends will, return
And at last my impatience will, be rewarded
And I, will be, another year older
And again my heart will, sing and sigh in the same
moment.

This Life Has No Title.

This life
It comes and arrives without a title ,a book, a chapter,
and a verse with which
To teach, dictate, or guide.
It arrives with no title
No poem, no prose, no rhyme
No words written upon the paper
No thoughts upon the babies mind.
This life arrives with empty moments, a void, a space,
a span
Waiting to be filled with life's experiences
To give it a fullness, a roundness, a solidity
An abundance, vivacity, exuberance
For anything we like to decide;
From tainted blackness, garbage, jealousy, and
imperfections
And a searching that will give it meaning,
understanding, purpose, and significance,
And for this we will look all our lives.
And in despondency, we will cry, shake our fists, and
ask why we were denied,
The satisfaction of becoming our true selves, the
person we wanted to be, the real me
To the unfulfilled
To the emptiness of the hollow grave.

We Are All But Flowers

We are all but flowers
We seed
We germinate
We grow
We bloom
We wither
We die
We seed
We are all but flowers
In the warm sun
With our upturned faces.

We are all but flowers
Weeping in the rain
With our bowed heavy heads
We stand and sway
As if in pain
And as we stand
We in our loneliness and loveliness
Wish that some gentle hand
Would pluck us up
Caress us
And marvel at our beauty.

Miscellany

In Any Street

In any street the concrete grows
Between the houses row on row
This marks our place
And in the sky
The metal birds do swiftly fly
Scarce heard amid the din below.

We will soon be dead
Now with not too many days to go
Lived life, felt warmth,
Saw the evening go
Heeded not what we were meant to heed
And now we lie in any street.

Take up our quarrel with the governments that never
listen
And are always saying no
To you from failing humanity we throw
The light, the mantle to hold high
For faith has been broken with us
And now we die in any street.

Pills

A pill for this
A pill for that
A pill for another bug attack.
A pill for headaches
And period pains
Pills for love
And elimination

Pills to satisfy the whole nation
Pills to stop
Pills to start
Pills to make you fart
Pills for your heart
Pills for sex
Pills to pep up your pex

Pills for the baby
Pills just because maybe
Pills for hit and miss
Pills to make you piss
Pills for your cold
Pills to stop you becoming old!
Pills to stop you smoking

Pills to stop you choking
Pills to give you an erection
Pills to give you hair
Pills to make you dare
Pills to stop you wheezing
Pills to stop you sneezing
Pills to make you wild

Pills to make you mild
Pills to make you sick
Pills to make you shit
Pills to stop spots
Pills to stop clots
Pills to make you thin
Pills to make you sin

Pills for the perfect skin
Pills to make you win
Pills for excuses, excuses for pills
Pills to give you thrills
Pills to give you the will
Pills to make you brave
Pills that make you misbehave!

Pills for the mind
Pills to reduce your behind
Pills to make you lie
Pills to make you cry
Pills to make you feel good
Pills to make you wish you could
Pills to stop you eating
Pills to stop you cheating.

Pills that make you go on and on and on and on and
on and on...

Well so ya think.

Similar Person

Have you ever noticed wherever you go
There's always someone you think you know
That someone with that familiar face
But you can't quite remember the place

You last saw a bloke like that over there
Sitting in that chair.
He's got the same walk
And by all accounts he's got the same talk

And when he sat for lunch
He had the same round shouldered hunch
He even used his fork the same way
And the flickering of his eyes held the same charm
and play.

His hands extend in much the same gesture
Maybe he thinks he's some court jester.
And on his fingers he wore a few pretentious rings
And by the look of him in his heart he hid a few sins.
But, don't we all!

Have you ever noticed wherever you go
There is always some one you think you recognise
Though from where you don't quite know
It could be some place you visited long ago

With a friend or old school chum
Or with some one with whom you had a bit of fun,
Who was that? I can't remember the name!
Oh, isn't that a shame, a naughty shame.

Have you ever noticed wherever you go
There is always someone you think you know
Though you can't quite remember from which place,
Because everyone you meet seems to have this
familiar face.

Pen To Paper

What happens when one cannot put pen to paper
As you know the thoughts should glide
And flow
Like the ink itself
It is not the pens nib that's rough
Nor is it the papers surface, for
It is I who cannot achieve the smooth
Unruffled motion
Of pen to paper.

Mother Love

A Mother's Lot

Mother's lot
Hot
At the cooker
I wonder what life's like for a hooker.
Mother's day
Delay
All the time
I feel like turning to a life of crime.
Mother easy
Carefree
Could someone just fuck me.
Mother's heaven
Legs eleven
Just spread me on the bed
And kiss around the head.
Mother perfect
Disinfectant
Clean
I have a fantasy
A dream.
By and by mother weeds
Concedes
Someone mop my brow
I feel like a stressed out dairy cow
Being milked at the washing up sink
Daily, of my sap and pleasure.
Surely a mother is a thing to treasure.

Mother perfect
Mother dream
Mother lovely
Mother always seen.

Mother

I'm just a mother,
That's what I am
A mother
Who nurtures
And caters
For whims and demands
Who understands needs
In between all this I pull a few weeds
Now and again administer a few caring words
Antiseptic cream
And a band-aid.

I am the doctor
The thinker
The philosopher
I am the one who puts and holds it all together
I wear many hats
Which are many things
All in one day
And in the same moment
I can change from a kitten, a pussycat,
To a tigress.

My hands do dishes
And cook up delicious wishes
Which go from oven
To plate
On to palate
Then back to dishes
Then everything comes around the same
Suddenly I am brought back from deep thought
"Mummy, Mummy, Mummy" my child insistently
pleads,
Tugging upon my skirt.
"Can I have a kiss?" he asks with sweet delight.
How can I refuse.
Do you know something
Through all this
This is the reward
A wonderful reward.

Eternal

This is the eternal
It sits upon every mothers lap.
This is the eternal that explains all
And cannot be discounted or denied
By tests or written words
Or by the tests of beasts of men.
For this is the eternal
It sits upon every mothers lap.

Gifts To A Child

I'll make to you a gift of thoughts
To put inside your head.
I'll make to you a gift of imagination
To create in you a fascination.
I'll make to you a gift of visions
To give you colourful prisms.
I'll make to you a gift of openness
That floats upon a thoughtful ocean, motion and bliss.
I'll make to you a gift of strong will and strength
To carry you through the ups and downs, which at length
Will make you stronger still.
I'll make to you a gift of dreams
Pulled so tightly together at the seams.
I'll make to you a gift of life
To be cherished at any price.
I'll make to you a gift of understanding, of questions
All in a mere suggestion.
I'll make to you a gift of things that can be done
And make you realise
That in one day you can become
And see
All the words that come from me.

Tea Time

Washing up
Is all I do,
Scraping dishes
One and two,
Cooking meals,
And making wishes,
Of noodles, rice
And all things nice.
Pouring from packets fresh-frozen vegetables,
Oh no, I forgot to read the label.
I make the food nice and clean,
I fry, I poach,
I boil, and steam.
Yummy, for tea we have tasty loach.
Eat the food,
Nice and polite
Not crude,
With manners all perfect in style.
Then we sit in contentment for a while,
Happy in our investment,
Rubbing our tummies.
'Oh, thank you mummy
For my tea.'

My son says, now sitting on his father's knee;
He tells him of his special day,
Of all the wild things he did at play,
Suddenly, in mid conversation,
He changes direction.
'Where's my chocolate?'
Ah, father laughs, 'I knew you could not wait,
Alright my son,
You can have, some,
Then it's bath, book, and bed.'

My Boy

I love to hear him on the phone
Especially when I'm on business away from home
I love to hear his little voice
You could say I almost rejoice;
At the thought of being back home with my son
For me he is the only one
Who fills that special place in my heart
And gives my day a worthwhile start.

Old Age

A Place Of Old Things

The darkness of the night fails me now
As does my sight
And the rest of the day is carried away
By some other force, though I know not what.
Now, I am eighty
I should be in a place of antiquities
On a shelf of shambled things in some album
Forever printed on a grey faded photograph
All tattered and torn at the edges without hope;
Of a stranger's hand sticking it together with tape.
Yet, more pleasure is to be had by unknown fingers
And questioning eyes that come to touch and muse
At the expressions within the faded photograph
Often to marvel at the odd fashions
And giggle at the restraining values of our youth.

My lands end up as if on a market stall
Waiting for the highest bid,
My hands being tied
My speech being slurred
Caused by the drugs on my brain,
Thus I am unable to regain what is rightfully mine.
My life, disappears down the plug hole
With no hope of recycling me
From behind locked doors (a place society calls home)
We are left
To walk through the archives of our mind

Struggling and determined to remember the calm
quiet times.
Some things others will never take away or ever know
Or have the pleasure of knowing some secret thing
that happened long ago
Nor will it end up in a place of old things.

Though it would be much preferred to the chants,
wails,
And pitiful cries of our fellow citizens
All suffering the same indignities
By the same uncaring hands.
Youth and age do not always click together
As do keys in locks.
But no matter what the time is
We should always take a look at the clock,
That hangs, stands, or leans against the wall
In some familiar room or hall
And watch the seconds disappear
Not returning year by year.
The brightness of eternal day calls me now
No longer do I wander in the darkness of night
But in a place of old things that comfort my returning
sight.

Old Men

Old men still have dreams
Dreams of singing songs
And putting right the wrongs.
Old men still want to climb mountains
And enjoy youths fountain.
Old men still want to love
And not give it the elbow, the shove.
Old men still have ambition
And want to feel as though they still have a mission.
They want to be respected
And not ridiculed, or detested
For having heavy wrinkles
And saggy skin that crinkles.
Old men still want closeness and cuddles
And not to hear the words that confuse or befuddle.

Old men still have needs, wants, and desires
And still feel passions hot fires.
Old men that went off to the great wars
Still want things the same as they were before
But understand that this can be no more
Even though, they, still given the chance would love
to explore.

Old men still want to pen and scribble
And not be left in a winged chair
With only a nurse to wipe away the dribble
Or left to stare
With no one to care.
Old men still have a heart
But realise that they are almost back at the start
At their meeting place, their zenith,
Where life to them only now becomes worth more
than a penn'orth.

Now

I am an old lady now
Sitting by the window now
Looking out from my imprisoned world now
With an imprisoned view now
With no one to speak with now
Unable to get my words out now
Each day I sit and watch my life now
Not worth much now
Waiting for the gate to open now
So I can escape the here and now, now

I was once a daughter
A woman
A mother
A grandmother
An aunt
A friend
But now
I am nothing now
Just flesh and bone now
Waiting for my end now.

Remote

Old men sit quietly remote
Waiting for winter's coat
But now that September has gone
They wait to sing the eternal song
Men that were once bold and strong
Sit in the shadows long
Of the late late day
Frittering their moments away.
As the dark side before death approaches
Blackness encroaches.
And fragments of rank and order
That did once applaud her
Dissipate as if a mist
Into a life's final twist
Of thoughtless scattered thoughts
Where the connection may now end and begin, and
begin and end.
Remote and distant
Far and away
Unresolved, dissolved,
Left and gone,
Not coming back
No return.
Now back to enemy deserts, remote
With not a thing to think about
Barren.

One Life Only

Are You Where You Want To Be

Are you where you want to be
Are you on the right track
Have you journeyed and laboured
Only to be in the same place
To be stabbed in the back?
Are you held down by your own thoughts
And procrastinations
Or by the mouths of others
Do you go along with masses
And never have any ideas of your own?
Do you question the words and articles
Which are written every day
You know, the ones that brainwash the positive
thoughts away?
You can be what you want to be
There is nothing you cannot be
It's just the argument you have with yourself every
day
You know the one that goes on inside your head
That gets in the way,
And stops you being you.

Debate Debate Debate

Debate about this
Debate about what we all might miss
Debate about that
Debate about HRH hats
Debate about big brother
Debate about some one having a bit of the other
Debate about some poor bloody cat
Left to starve in some filthy flat
Debate about road rage
Debate about retirement age
Debate about wrinkles
Debate about curtains with crinkles
Debate about silicone boobs
Debate about space age loos
Debate about skin cancer and the sun
Debate about a child with a gun
Debate about keeping London's streets neat
Debate about CJD and meat

Debate about NHS
Debate about VHS
Debate about IVF
Debate about HIV
Debate about Viagra
Debate about hormones
Debate about the pill
Debate about us all having our fill
Debate about starvation

In some far off nation
Debate about child labour
Debate about doing the Government a favour
Debate about political correctness
Debate about the next summit
Debate about the last seven generations
environmental mess
Debate about the next seven generations
environmental mess
Debate about someone else's wife
Debate about someone else's life

Debate always about someone else's business
Debate about bitterness.
Debate about the beginning of the day
Debate every hour
Debate all the time
Debate about crime
Debate about the rain,
Debate about the bloody same
Debate about myocardial infarction
Debate about labial reduction
Debate about liposuction
Debate about collagen injection
Debate about the powder snow.
Debate about people with nowhere to go.
Debate about life's ebbs and flow
Debate about someone saying yes,
Debate about someone saying no
Debate Debate Debate

Burning

Burning burning
Upon the stake
Shoeless my toes
Smoke in my nose
Eyes peep blind
Though I realise I will die
My spirit will fly
Into the sky
I will be fried.

Newman Michaels

Don't Steal My Dreams

Don't steal my dreams
Because I won't ever steal yours
Don't put me down
Because I want to be something different.
Don't laugh and ridicule me
Because you don't understand me
Don't rub salt into the wounds
To insult the injury any more
Just because you think you might even the score.
Don't wipe away my dreams on the floor
Or throw them in bin bags out the back door
I'll never do that to you.
In fact, I'll never laugh at anything you want to do
Or throw water on your goals and inspirations
I'll never treat your dreams as if they were weeds
Dreams don't deserve to end up on the compost heap.
So the next time you want to laugh at me
Take a look at what you do
And question the way in which you understand
The things that you see.

Every Enjoyable Puff

The cigarette smoke swirled about my face,
Blinding me
Blackening my lungs
With every enjoyable puff.
This most unsociable habit
Causes much displeasure
And disapproval.
'Don't see why we have to put up with smoking in the
office,' some say.
'It really is offensive
Having to inhale other people's breath'

'We quite agree,' said the others
'But, you don't have to work here with us,
As we don't have to work with you,
Let me give you some food for thought,'
Said the smoker.
'Every time you fart you pollute the atmosphere
Every time your car engine roars, splatters, and fumes
into action
Or you spray your hair into style,
You are doing more harm than any smoker could.'

How Many Times

How many times did you phone me
Write or come around to see me
For anything at all
When I was not famous at all.
How many times did you speak with me
Love me
Ask me
And chat with me
Never.
Because I was no one at all.
But now I am famous
And known by one and all
You think you can boss me
Talk and shout at me
Insult me
And chastise me
But, alas you cannot
Because I am not
The person you want me to be.

Knock On The Door

If you don't knock on the door
It will never open.
If you don't pick up the phone
It will never ring.
If you don't make that contact
You'll never move on.
If you don't buy a new broom
You'll never make a clean sweep.
If you don't push yourself forward
You'll never achieve your reward.
And if you don't see your dreams
You'll never understand the vision.

Knocked Down

I once was poor
But now I'm not
I learned to get up
When I got knocked down
I learned to brush myself off
And walk away
Thinking to myself
Tomorrow is another day.

At times I found it hard to take the knocks
And bear the disappointment
But I got back up
And walked away
Thinking to myself
Tomorrow is another day
And each time I got back up
I become more resilient.

And began to smile to myself
Knowing at last that I could become my real self
And that my dreams
Would not be left on a shelf, forgotten.
So if you get knocked down
Get back up and walk smiling away
Because tomorrow is another day,
Tomorrow is your day.

The Telly

Step by step you'll get there,
Just as long as you sit in your lazy boy chair;
Night after night
Your life will be stolen away
In front of the telly.
Hour by hour you'll sit there in quiet discontent
Wishing you had done this and that
Putting off what you should have done today
Till tomorrow, next week and, never.
Step by step you'll get there alright
Without having done what you set out to do,
All because you sat in front of the telly
Your dreams turned to jelly
And just melted away.
Do you really want to spend the rest of your life this
way?

No

No sun
Only winter
No shagging
No protection
No smoking
No choking
No spitting
No coughing
No parking
No shagging

No loitering
No protesting
No striking
No opinions
No trespassing
No peeping
No stopping
No popping
No swinging
No shagging

No phoning
No knocking
No blocking
No selling
No logging
No picnicking

No rubbish
No whispering
No showing
No shagging

No opposition
No argument
No political notion
No commotion
No emotions
No slowing
No crying
No begging
No confrontation
No shagging

No multiplication
No manipulation
No questions
No reasoning
No thoughts
No walking this way
No running
No shunting
No bunting
No shagging

No leaving doors open
No showing the way
No hoping

No dreaming
No scheming
No wants
No greed
No needs
No good seeds
No shagging

No discontentment
No resentment
No enhancement
No advancement
No voice
No leading the way
No choice
No shaking the stick
No eating the carrot
NO !!!!! no control.

The Fat In My Fridge

No food
in my fridge
But only fat
No food
in my cupboard
But only fat
No food at the Supermarket,
But only fat
No food in my life
But only fat.

Today, we are taught to hate the fat
But do you really want to live your life like that?
Today we are taught that fat is not good,
But who really cares about what we shouldn't
and should.
Because one hundred years from now we will ALL be
dead
All laid to rest in our
death beds,
And who will really give a fuck about what we ate
Is it going to ruin a nation or a state?

I like fat with my cheese and jam
I love ketchup with my ham
I love chips with everything
I love fat because of the full feeling it brings.
So, I am not going to listen to what the experts say,

For I CANNOT
live my life that way
their way.
I don't give a shit about the calories,
I want to live my life with fatness in the food with
ease.

I must have some fun;
While I enjoy a really creamy dreamy yummy bun.
I cannot live without the chocolate,
Nor for that matter can my mates, it is a social thing.
So whatever the fat in my fridge doth bring
I am going to be me, not you,
And not be the someone acceptably thin and new
Just for the media,
Who think they have the right to tell
everyone to live their lives in tedium.

So, before you make a judgement on me
You cannot tell me, that at midnight
When you come home from the pub all pissed and
tight
That you have never gone to the fridge in the kitchen
Itching
To find some food with some fat,
Which is not,
Thin,
Anorexic,
Tasteless or Flat.

Our Planet

A Simple Answer

It is simple,
Is it not?
That you should laugh
While the earth just rots.
It is important
Is it not?
That the earth should fester
And you should not.
It is justice
Is it not?
That the earth should die
And you should not.
It is the truth
Is it not?
That all is finished
And you are not.
It is simple
Is it not?
How simple the answers can be
Is it not?

Black Dawn

A danger to us all
A clone will be
You mark my words
You take note of the words that come from me.
These clone beasts
Will make us their feasts
You'll pass them in the road
Town and street
You'll walk behind their feet
And not know them.
You won't see the seam or hem
You won't hear them tick
They'll never get sick
They'll never break down
You'll never know what goes on beneath their gowns,
Beneath their suits.
Do you compute?
They'll never be affected by the sun
Now, that man has held to his head a gun.

One day you'll wake up and
Whilst you sip tea from a cup
You'll see a thousand clones on your lawn
And this will be the beginning of the black dawn.
Do you compute?
For I see the future in my head
And as you lie in your weary bed
My words shall come to mind
They will come, and haunt, and find,
And, you will remember the words I wrote,
The words you first thought so remote,
The words you first thought were out of tune,
The words that now swirl around your room,
Because you know that the black dawn is near.
So before you laugh and throw my words in the bin,
Man, now needs to take a look within,
For he knows the words I speak are true,
Now, he must seek the answers,
Before is left on this earth are few.
Do you compute?

The Perfect World

The world should be revolving in harmony
But it's not.
It should be clip-clopping down the road
Like an escaped horse
But it's not.
It should be a brand new day every day
But it's not.
One thing it sure is not
Is a happy place
On equal terms with it is the human race.

As it spreads its malice like a poison
All for the want of greed;
The rain forests disappear
Along with a million other things
For pulp paper,
Or pleasant ivory decorations.
What a pleasant sport the human race is.
"Come on chaps let's see what's fair game today"
Man, should be doing good.

Black Shore

May the winds of war
Not blow too long
For death is weak
And life's too strong
May the sins of man
Be but a speck
Before we make this earth a wreck.

May the tree of life
Bring fruit not strife
Over every land
Before it is ruined by man's hand.
And the ebbing tide
Be man's pride
Not a black shore
Beating at the devils door.

Lights on the Landscape

Unlike the lights on the landscape
Man shall fade and die
And where he stood
His mark will be forever etched upon this earth,
An unpleasant picture of his lack of
Compassion and incompatibility with everything;
From the mysterious beckoning of the night sky
To the unfathomable depths of the oceans
There will no lighting up time for him,
No gift from heaven
No extended hand at the gate no eternal peace.

Unlike the lights on the landscape
He shall become a dark shadow
Leaving his poison smog
To caress and kill;
All the old
And all the new;
Life
Will be choked to death
A beautiful birth drawing its last breath
A babe wrapped in a shroud
Swaddled in the arms of failure.

But in all probability
He will deny his infallibility
Being certain of living forever
Taking all that the landscape has to offer,

Yet spending many a moment in discord
With his surroundings
Wishing he could do without it
Wishing he could do without that
He will never live without the land
But it can
And will live without him.

Unlike the lights on the landscape
Man will fade
And die
A beautiful birth
A gift from heaven
For an earthly Mother
Will draw its last polluted breath
Out of the fetid air
There will be no remorse
Just the comfort of knowing, that
He will have escaped his filthy existence.

The War Machine

Men with charms
In arms
Men in fine fettle
Encased in metal
Men in strategic fight
Night after night
Up in the sky
Some will ask why.

In a place with no flowers
And in the heavy bombardment of showers
Men with social graces
Are camped out in bases
Under tents
Paying no rents
At tables eating
Mentally giving the enemy a beating.

Men in camouflage,
Anticipating another barrage
Of enemy fire
Wishing it was love and desire
A woman with all her sex
And feminine complex.
But, this is the war machine
And she is just another dream.

But now the men are spent
With no time to repent
Men shot down from clouds
Ready for shrouds
In a place with no flowers
And in the heavy bombardment of showers
Life, is lost in another land,
In the bloodied sand.

The Animals in the Zoo

The animals in the Zoo
They stare out at you
Forlornly from their cages
Watching from eyes that hold no hope or glimmer
With sad heavy hearts
And pent up rages.

Habitually pacing from corner to corner day after day
Following a well trodden track
Always in the same direction, going nowhere
Some howl out continuously for their lost mates, soulfully
Roaring for the wilderness
That calls them back.

The beautiful animals
Call out to you
As you walk past their bright glass enclosures
And with heavy heart, we sigh heavily
Knowing that on our return next year
Not a thing will have changed.

The animals in the Zoo
They look at you with dull eyes
Trust unquestionably your decisions
From their prisons
They give to your thoughts food
Their situation a wrenching of the gut.

The animals in the Zoo
They stare out at you
From between steel bars, locked up
Safe, from harm, safe from where you took them.
Safe from where they are really meant to be
Being a spectacle always for the likes of you and me.

Man Will Eat The Fish Of It

Savage man
Making a vile sea
A boiling fermenting place
Of death

A savage sea it may be at times
To man and his many vessels
But a time bomb
He makes of it:

With every day that passes
He throws in his poison waste
He does not want it in his back yard
Nor on his precious immaculate lawn

But, he will eat the fish of it
And again the cycle begins
Flushed down the loo, out
Through the drains into the sewers

Then out into the streams, rivers, canals
Then back to the sea again
Where fish will eat the food of it
Then man will eat the fish of it.

To Some Men

To some men
The ultimate sin
Is to throw a fiver in the bin
But what about the bird you locked in a cage
By rights the whole world should be enraged;
Because you killed it when it did not sing
So you threw it in the bin.
It's not a fiver.
It's not the ultimate sin.
The money or your life.
The money or the bird.

And what of the dog you chained
Beat and probably maimed
When it messed on your carpet
And because of your anger
It was left to hunger
To starve, till its flesh hung from every bone,
Then you booted it out of your home,
Threw it in the bin.
It's not a fiver.
It's not the ultimate sin.
The money or your life.
The money or the dog.

And what of the horse
You hobbled and flogged
When you could not break its spirit.

It knew your weakness.
So you shot it between the eyes,
Then tossed it to frenzied dogs,
Threw it in the bin.
It's not a fiver.
Not the ultimate sin.
The money or your life.
The money or the horse.

And what of the rabbit and rat
In their laboratory homes
Where needles for this and that are stuck into their
skin
For testing this and testing that
Just so man can take another drug
To kill off another bug.
And all this in the name of scientific sin.
And now their lives are spent
They are thrown in the bin.
It's not a fiver.
Not the ultimate sin.
The money or your life.
The money or the rabbit and rat.

And what of the pig
Living in his crate
He knows his fate
At the end of a butcher's knife,
Anything is better than his life
He will happily accept his death,

It's his time to escape the clutches of man.
His life was in the bin before it started.
It's not a fiver.
Not the ultimate sin.
The money or your life.
The money or the pig.

Wise Words

"What we do to our earth,
We eventually do to ourselves
We are not the makers of earth
We are merely specks of dust in the soil
And what we do to that soil
We will eventually do to ourselves"

Lines inspired by Chief Seattle 1854 - a respected native
American Chief 'now'

Sadness

He Moves Beside You

Now that he is gone from you
His spirit moves beside you like a ghost
His presence shall be felt as a pleasant breeze
Across your face
A soft kiss upon your neck
A light stroke upon your hand
A butterfly fluttering by
A velvety furnishing enveloping you
A flower capturing the sunlight
Its perfume faintly assailing your senses
His presence shall be as real as the dawn's early light
As protective as an angel in the night
As the night's dark cold holds you tight
He is beside you in peaceful ease
Always.

In Slumber

I came to lay flowers at her feet
As she lay there in her eternal sleep
Her beauty was once a perfect dream
And to me even now she did seem
To be there
Sitting next to me on the chair.
I felt her whispering words caress my ears
As I remembered all the years
I had known her well
She had a heart as big as a bell
That would ring out a glorious tune
As if on a beautiful wedding day in hot June.

I am sure I felt her hand glide across my arm, as if to
Soothe my tortured soul with her usual calm,
reassuringly
Seeming to comfort me in my worry;
 She said,
'Life goes by at a hurry.
So when you come again to lay flowers at my feet
Do not weep
For I am at peace now
Because, when I was in pain
I could not imagine how
I would ever get as peaceful a sleep again
In slumber'.

My Friend

Time has come for my friend
His life is almost at an end
Time for him to say goodbye
And more than once I shall ask why;
As his pale bones are graced in flames
I'll remember all those silly games
And when his body the flames have charred
I'll hang his soul high in the sky
On a string of stars
Where the end and time will never die.

Sun-kissed

With my friend
Faith
Hope
Love
Charity
All died
And now every body will be denied her;
All encompassing love
Her gift of giving
Along with her peace and tranquillity
And calm, of mind and spirit.
Her presence will be forever missed
Sun-kissed.

On Going To My Best Friend's Grave

My friend at last is laid to rest
Gone is she at the Lord's behest,
And now I stand at the foot of her grave,
With my emotions all a whirl thinking of the love
she so unselfishly gave

With big tears in my dark sad eyes
I ask the Lord for his reasons and why, why,
He took her from everyone and all,
What was the whole point of it all?
Why take her away from the many who loved her

The many who were comforted by her
In their hour of need;
She planted in them a good seed
That would one day grow into hope and inspiration,
And be remembered with heartfelt affection.

These are the words from me to my friend
Who now lives in a small box,
(And now, as if dust, Her self, Her life,
Will run through my tightly clasped hands between
my quivering fingers
Away on a winnowing wind.)

Next to a small wooden cross
On a sunny grassy plot
In the corner of an allocated lot
Amongst cold hard headstones
Of her new found friends.

And I, in my warmth of life,
Shall stand and sigh
And sing and cry
And wonder always about her
Until my END.

The Bloom

You are my beginning
And I your end
And in between there was no middle
No nothing, no stem
Our lives were as imperfect flowers
With only the root and the bloom,
Because the stem was infested, infected, and twisted
It could not grow
And was eaten away;
In the cold harsh sunlight of day.
There was seed
But now there is only this beauty.
You were the root
And I am, the bloom.

There was no soil to nourish the stem,
Ever,
No water to quench its thirst,
At all
No one person to admire its captivating spirit
Or its passion to enthral.
And only now does my scent escape me
To bathe
And caress
In the glorious Summer sun.
You were the root
And I *am* the bloom
With a warmth
That remains still.

Walking In The Wild Wind

The wild wind flung itself around my head
Running amok through every strand of my hair
Pressing its well known presence into my depression.
And a black sky rose twice from a bush top
Where two black crows sat and crowed and crowed
Like two black witches having a wicked chat
Their timing perfect in every detail
I could almost understand what they had to say
Two black witches laughing in their usual wild way
Come to think of it as wild as the day
With each and every moment belonging to the other.
Walking in a wild wind
On a wild day
Trying to sort out the wildness in my head
Whilst walking in the wild wind.

The Human Touch

I'm not looking for anything much
Just a friend with a human touch,
Someone with that special feeling
To help me through with whatever I am dealing.
But sometimes I think that this I do not deserve
And that my voice will never be heard,
And at times like this I feel quite alone
Even in a crowd I feel on my own.
I am not asking for much
Just a special friend with a gentle touch
To help me heal the hurt inside.

Time

Buy Time

Time went by
As quick as the flicker of an eye.
By time?
All the time.
Buy time?
Never.

Copper Days

There it stood,
Quite noticeably in the corner of the kitchen,
Wasting much needed space;
As I remember,
Mother always kept it sparkling clean,
A day's work it would be for her
Copper day
It was wash day
Monday.

Fragments Of Time

You cannot throw them away fragments of time
Like pieces of paper in the bin
When the life you lead does not come up to your
expectations.
You cannot crush and crumple time in your hands
Like screwed up balls of paper
You cannot set time on fire
Time is alive.
It was not different today
In length or hour
It has always been the same
It never waits.

It never looks back at things
It never stops for laughter
It does not stop for love
It does not stop to influence
It makes no decisions,
This perfect elemental.
It does not argue with a situation
It cannot help circumstances
It cannot talk
It does not move from place to place
It is in every place.

It cannot see the dark of night
It cannot feel the warmth of the day
It never reaches any conclusion
It does not interfere with justice injustice
It has no hands with which to hold
It cannot cry
It has no foundation
It does not wear the jewels of earth
It is a jewel of earth.
It cannot read
It cannot write.

It cannot count the days, weeks, months or years
It cannot conduct itself in a corrupt manner
It cannot eliminate the atrocities of man
It cannot undo his malice, greed, and contempt.
Fragments of time
Ticking away to the end of the line
Ticking each second away with a chime
Ticking every moment away in your fragmented mind
Wasting it away, what a crime.
And every moment you live, Fragments,
Will run through your fingers as if in a sieve.

I See

I see time in the matter of an hour
I see time in the beauty of a flower
I see time in giving to a man a wife
I see time giving life.
I see a time when we are all sharing
But that will not happen till we are all caring
I see time waiting to go by
I see time ready and waiting, never to die.

Only Form

If you were to watch and wait for time to fly by,
You would not see it in its form.
But in the day, dusk, night and, dawn
You would see it in its only form.

Slow

Time went by
Like the clouds in the sky
Slow, so we thought
Yet, another minute in this glorious sun is all we sought
But as usual time went by at the same speed
Just in time to germinate another weed.

Take Time

Don't push time through the doors
Through the wall
Through the windows and floors
Just because things may not be going your way
Don't push it.
Time has its own speed
And moves constantly
And consistently
No faster
No slower.
Just take time to move through your day
And enjoy it all the way.
Have patience,
Take time.

Wild Nature

Fly On The Wall

I am a fly on the wall
And each day
I am treated to tears laughter and all;
Whilst watching every little thing you do
'And my,' I say to myself
'I'm glad I don't live in your shoes
I'd rather carry on licking and vomiting
On your meat and jam
Or making maggots to eat your ham
Or laying eggs on the cat's food in the hall'.
I am the fly on the wall
And each day I am treated
To newspapers
Sprays
Fly swats
And all
But I've survived the lot
And I'll outlive them all.

Rain All Day

Rain in drops
Rain in plops
Rain in splishes
Rain in splashes
Rain in lashes
Rain in crashes
Rain in beatings
Rain in sleetings
Rain threshing
Rain refreshing
Rain in a dark cloud
Rain in a mystical shroud
Rain onto flower rushes
Rain onto petal crushes
Rain in drips
Rain in tips
Wet rain
Fat rain
Thin rain
Drizzly rain
Squally rain
Rain drops horizontally
Rain drops vertically
Rain drops onto mountain's top
Rain drops never stop.

Storm Calm

Waves crashing
White horses foaming
Wind so gusty
Boats rocking
Waves dying
Wind calming
Storm going
No wind blowing
Waves stop crashing
White horses popping
Wind so calm
Boats stop rocking
All is calm
Storm is gone
Nothing is wrong.

Newman Michaels

The Land By The Sea

Go down to the land
The land by the sea
And listen to the wind
As it howls and sings
Swathing itself around your head
Like bandages in confusion
Or Medusa
Or tattered rags
That were once the ghost ship's flags.

Go down to the land by the sea
And listen to it
As it hisses and swishes
Swathing itself around your ears
Like venomous snakes
Or Medusa
Or twisting eels
Caught in the albatrosses beak

Go down to the land by the sea
And listen to the shells
As they voice their opinion
Swathing their thoughts around your mind
Like tentacles in a swirling sea
Or Medusa
Or vines in a storm.

Go down to the land by the sea
And listen to the waves
As they rise and fall against the shore
Swathing their mysterious call
Around your good intentions
Like the jellyfishes poisoned tendrils
Or Medusa
Or shredded ropes scattered
And blowing about the sand.

Go down to the land
The land by the sea
And let it
Let it
Beckon, beckon, beckon, beckon, beckon, beckon.

The Sea

The never ever sea
Basks in the sunshine
And equally the cold
Ageless in time
It takes the young and old
And never ever repents
It goes on so bold
The sea that folds and creases and mounts
Swings in mood
Between rock in and out
Up stones and dripping walls
Crashing into mists
That fog, and shell.

The never ever sea
A merciless grey hell
Living a swirling swell
Always in ceaseless motion
Locomotion commotion
Seething heaving
Never leaving
A stone unturned
Always churned
Never concerned
About any loss
Dross
Could not give a toss.

And now the never ever sea
Sleeps so serene
All a perfect a sheen
An alluring dream
Spiteful
Insightful
Mindful
Of everything
Every sting
Frill
And thrill.
Softly as it awakes upon the pebbles on the shore
It whispers.

The Snow Flake

The snow falls like a ballerina
It puts on a perfect show
As small as an ant
It is still weather
It feels like velvet
But it is still water.
Sometimes hail
Sometimes rain
On the window pane
Sometimes big
Sometimes small
But still, it is snow after all.

Newman Michaels

Woman

A Poem For Me

Ironing, I've got stacks of it
But who cares!
It is time to sit
To write a poem
Story, or rhyme,
While I've got the time,
And the lines are still in my head.

I know the floor needs a clean,
But first I need to dream
Of a bright hot and sunny beach
Where I shall sit,
And for once the world can wait for me,
Where I can be myself,
And blow the dirty cups

That need to be put on the dishwasher shelf.
I want to feel the warmth on me
The sun on my skin,
And the sea that lovingly caresses the shore
Stirring my thoughts.
I don't want to make another bed,
I just want the perspiration

To run between my glistening breasts,
I want to feel the woman within,
And be the woman within, without.
I don't want to peel another spud, or carrot
I just want to sit on the beach
To write a few lines, poems, or prose,
In Brisbane, I suppose.

A Woman's Day

Fat day
Thin day
Slim belly day
Swollen belly day
Sexy day
Horny day
Pissed off day
Happy day
Rushing day
Fed up day
Nice day
Glorious sun on my skin day
Having a good day
Won the lottery day
No more work for me any day
Dreamy day.

In A Woman's Eyes

In a woman's eyes,
You'll see anguish, pain and lies,
You'll see disgust, want and devastation,
You'll see appeasement, love and happiness,
And sad moments
That will not be denied.
You'll see deepness unparalleled,
Tears welled.
You'll see heartache and betrayal.
You'll see promises care and understanding,
You'll see indifference, difference,
All wrapped up in bandages,
Plasters,
And intravenous feed from outside.

You'll see all this wrapped up in a beautiful
expression,
And a lovely smile.
You'll see long lost depths unfathomable.
You'll see stories of tales untold,
Of admiration,
And disintegration.
You'll see life's biggest mystery,
In life sold,
In a single moment,
And as singular as the day or night,
Along the lonely road,
You'll see things you wish you had not seen,

But they'll be there all the same.
In a woman's eyes
You'll see desire, compassion,
Passion,
All wrapped up in what you perceive before you.
In a woman's eyes
You'll see many nights of tenderness,
And you'll swear you saw all her complexities
revealed,
But they'll be there all the same.
You'll swear you heard the music,
Felt the shift,
Felt the mountains move,
But they'll be there all the same
In any given space and moment of time.

In a woman's eyes
You'll see given, giving,
Had and having,
All wrapped up in the shifting sands
Gently slipping away,
Being there all the same.

A Woman's Fullness

Sometimes I think that I am nothing
And alone
Unseen by mortal flesh
I feel that I am not a thing to be reckoned with
Until I perceive my full womb.
Which to fullness and nothingness does come
Where fruition and hope do appear
But this is not necessarily real
But from which there is not escape.
It affects the shape of the thoughts that live in my
mind
It affects the shape of my day
My full womb that empties and plays
Thoughtlessly and willingly all the same
Like each turning month
In some lunatic game.

The Womb Within

The womb within
The familiar alien
The womb with a mind of its own
On its own
Within me.
The womb with its own intelligence
Living its own life
And controversy
All the time
Without knowledge
And understanding of its host.
It lives deep down
And all the same up front
In my thoughts
And in my ingestion of the world that comes to me.
It creates another bad day;
As my body (whom you might think belongs to
someone else)
Swells more plump than the waves of the tidal sea,
With breasts that swing the sore see-saw,
And a maturing belly that looks about three months
pregnant.
All the time this familiar alien having control over me.
And now that I feel large and voluptuous,
Sexy even,
But I don't want to
Because to my mind I look fat.

Rosebud

One day I will sail away on my mind
Well at least for a time
A woman's time
To escape the here and now
The needs
The wants
The grace
The favours
I'll fling away all responsibilities
To capture just one small moment
That is mine,
In this life time.

I'll polish my nails
Shave off the unwanted hair
Put on something Sexy
That is me
Do a dance around a chair,
Then imagine
That I am young and sexually attractive
Standing proud
Ready for action
Anywhere, anyplace
Anytime with some young stud.
'Ha, Rosebud!'

I'll remember the feelings that once were
Then sadly, I'll sink in a heap
And weep a weep for every woman in the world
I'll feel the pain of every woman in the world
For every woman who wants to be loved: again,
For the very first time.
'Ha, Rosebud!'
But now my bloom of youth has gone
No one wants to look at me anymore
My age has come.
I want to live!
'Ha, Rosebud!'

Transform

Transform me into a beauty queen
Into something that no one else as ever seen
That no one else as ever been
Transform me into a perfect dream.

Give me a plastic face without a seam
Give my skin the perfect sheen
Make me sparkle, glisten and gleam.
Give me a body all taut and lean

To give me presence on the movie screen
As I don't want to live the life of a nobody in between
Or finish up as some has been.
I want people to understand I look like what I really
mean

And that I am not only human ugly, and obscene
Down some latrine
With laws of nature to contravene
The clean image of the imperfect human being.

Printed in the United Kingdom
by Lightning Source UK Ltd.
107523UKS00001B/187-210